George Washington Carver

the peanut scientist

Revised Edition

Patricia and Fredrick McKissack

Series Consultant
Dr. Russell L. Adams, Chairman
Department of Afro-American Studies, Howard University

Enslow Publishers, Inc.

40 Industrial Road	PO Box 38
Box 398	Aldershot
Berkeley Heights, NJ 07922	Hants GU12 6BP
USA	UK

http://www.enslow.com

To Margaret Emily Haskins

Revised edition of *George Washington Carver: The Peanut Scientist* © 1991

Library of Congress Cataloging-in-Publication Data

McKissack, Pat, 1944–
   George Washington Carver : the peanut scientist / Patricia and Fredrick McKissack—Rev. ed.
     p. cm. — (Great African Americans)
   Includes index.
   Summary: Simple text and illustrations describe the life and accomplishments of the scientist who promoted the idea of crop rotation and found many uses for peanuts.
   ISBN 0-7660-1700-1
   1. Carver, George Washington, 1864?–1943—Juvenile literature. 2. African American agiculturists—Biography—Juvenile literature. 3. Agriculturists—United States—Biography—Juvenile literature. 4. Peanuts—Juvenile literature. [1. Carver, George Washington, 1864?–1943. 2. Agriculturists. 3. African Americans—Biography.] I. McKissack, Fredrick. II. Title.
   S417.C3 M298   2001
   630'.92-dc2l
   [B]

                                                           2001003990

To Our Readers
We have done our best to make sure all Internet addresses in this book were active and appropriate when we went to press. However, the author and the publisher have no control over and assume no liability for the material available on those Internet sites or on other Web sites they may link to. Any comments or suggestions can be sent by e-mail to comments@enslow.com or to the address on the back cover.

Every effort has been made to locate all copyright holders of materials used in this book.
If any errors or omissions have occurred, corrections will be made in future editions of this book.

Illustration Credits: © Corel Corporation, p. 7; George Washington Carver National Monument, pp. 9, 21T; Library of Congress, pp. 4, 17; Moorland-Spingarn Research Center, Howard University, pp. 3, 22; National Archives, p. 27; National Archives and Records Administration, p. 21B; National Portrait Gallery, Smithsonian Institution, p. 16; Photographs and Prints Division, Schomburg Center for Research in Black Culture, The New York Public Library, Astor, Lenox and Tilden Foundations (background "frame" © Corel Corporation), p. 25; Photographs courtesy of the Simpson College Archives, Indianola, IA, pp. 6, 10–11, 12, 13, 15, 18, 20, 24, 26.

Cover Credits: Courtesy of the Simpson College Archives, Indianola, IA; George Washington Carver National Monument; Library of Congress; Moorland-Spingarn Research Center, Howard University.

TABLE OF CONTENTS

George Washington Carver
Born 1864(?)–January 5, 1943

CHAPTER 1

Stolen in the Night

oses and Susan Carver owned a small farm in Diamond Grove, Missouri. They owned one slave, Mary. She had two small children, James and George.

One day a neighbor came to warn the Carvers. Slave raiders were in the area. Slave raiders stole slaves and sold them again.

The raiders came late that night. They stole Mary and baby George and then rode away. Moses Carver went after them. He found baby

This statue is at the George Washington Carver National Monument in Diamond, Missouri. As a boy, George loved plants and animals.

George by the side of the road. He never found Mary.

The Carvers had no children. So they raised James and George as their own. The boys called the Carvers Aunt Susan and Uncle Moses.

George was a sickly boy. His voice was thin and weak. He stuttered sometimes when he spoke in a hurry. But he was a happy child who loved plants and animals.

Aunt Susan taught him to read and write. She gave him a Bible. He loved his Bible very much.

The boy was always full of questions. He wanted to learn about everything. But the only school for black children was miles away. It was too far for a little boy to walk each day. George had to wait.

George learned to read the Bible.

CHAPTER 2

Why? and How?

When George was about twelve years old, he left the Carvers. He wanted to go to school. He walked to Neosho, Missouri. A family found George sleeping in their barn. They let the boy live with them. George worked and went to Lincoln School.

A few years passed. George learned all he could at Lincoln. He heard about a school in Fort Scott, Kansas. So he moved there. Another family let George live with them. Soon, young Carver

George had
many
questions.
"I wanted to
know every
strange
stone, flower,
insect, bird,
or beast,"
he said.

was old enough to live on his own. For a while he moved from place to place.

Then he came to a small Kansas town. Another man named George Carver lived there. So George added a "W" to his name. "It is for Washington,"

At first, George, below, studied art and music. He wanted to be an artist.

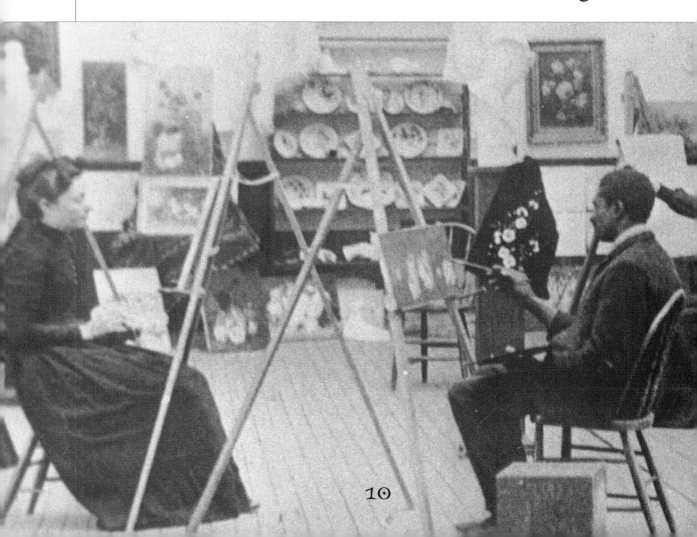

he told his friends. *George Washington Carver*—he liked the sound of his new name.

George wanted to go to college. Not many black men went to college in the 1890s. But George Carver was sure that he would go. He worked hard and saved his money.

2

When George started college, he was so poor that he lived in a shack.

At last Carver went to college in Iowa. There he studied what he liked best—plants and farming. Then he went to Iowa State College in Ames to study. He graduated in 1896. Still, there was much more he wanted to learn.

George Washington Carver would spend the rest of his life asking questions and looking for the answers. He was a scientist. And scientists are always asking Why? and How?

George was offered jobs at Iowa State and at Tuskegee Institute. It was hard to choose.

CHAPTER 3

Tuskegee Farm

eorge Carver was asked to stay at Iowa State and teach. But Booker T. Washington asked Professor Carver to come teach at Tuskegee Institute in Alabama.

The all-black school was started by Booker T. Washington in 1881. In 1896, Mr. Washington wrote a letter to Professor Carver: "Will you come to Tuskegee to teach?" Carver thought about it. Then he answered: "I am coming."

It was fall 1896 when Professor Carver went to

Tuskegee. He had thirteen students. His job was to teach science. But he had no lab. This didn't stop him. The class made a lab from things they found.

The school also had a farm. The soil was poor. The cotton plants were small and weak. Farmers in the South had been growing cotton on the land for many years. Professor Carver said, "The soil needs a rest." He and the class did a project. "We will not plant cotton," he said. "We will plant sweet potatoes." And they did.

Professor Carver said that learning skills like farming was "the key to unlock the golden door of freedom" for African Americans.

Carver and a student talk about plants.

**The students at Tuskegee helped to build their laboratory.
Carver is second from the right in this photo.**

The next year they grew cowpeas, another kind of vegetable. "The land has to rest," he said. So the third year they grew cotton again. That cotton crop grew bigger and stronger than before. Carver was one of the first scientists to teach crop rotation—growing different plants to make the soil better.

17

The boll weevil is a bug that eats cotton plants. In the early 1900s, boll weevils came into the United States from Mexico. Farmers were worried. What could they do? Carver told them to plant goobers! Boll weevils don't like goobers.

Carver the scientist was always busy in his lab.

18

CHAPTER 4

Plant Goobers!

Goobers!

Goober is an old African name for peanut. Slaves brought goobers from Africa. They grew them in small gardens. Goobers were mostly used to feed animals.

Farmers came to Tuskegee from all over the South. Professor Carver told them about his work. What can be done with peanuts? They are only good for hogs, people said. Carver found many

What could be done with all those peanuts?
Professor Carver had many ideas.

ways to use peanuts. His students liked peanut butter best.

Who will buy the peanuts? Professor Carver didn't know. But, as always, he kept looking for answers.

Then an idea came. The quiet professor asked a group of important businessmen to have dinner

with him. He served them
bread, soup, meat, cookies,
and ice cream.

Professor Carver wrote books to help farmers.

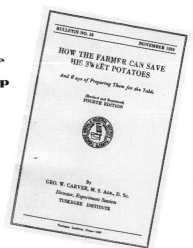

They all agreed that the food was
good—very good. Then Professor
Carver told them: Everything they had
eaten had been made with peanuts!
What a surprise!

Professor Carver was full of more surprises.
He showed the businessmen what they could make
from the peanuts. He
showed them why
they should buy
the farmers'
peanut crops.

Carver and his students built the Jesup Wagon, a traveling school

Carver prepared bread, soup, meat, cookies, and ice cream—and all were made of peanuts!

What he said made sense. Now the farmers could sell their crops.

It is no surprise that George Washington Carver was called the farmer's best friend.

CHAPTER 5

The Wizard of Tuskegee

George Washington Carver won many awards. Henry Ford, who made cars, gave him money to build a new lab. Every day scientists from many countries came to see the "Wizard of Tuskegee." Most of the time they found the small, quiet man working.

Professor Carver could have made lots of money. But owning things wasn't important to the great scientist. He owned only one suit. And he walked to his lab every day.

Although he had no wife or children, he was never alone. Tuskegee was home. His students were family. When Professor Carver wasn't working, he enjoyed reading the Bible that Susan Carver had given him long ago.

People had lots of questions for Professor Carver. He got piles of mail.

The kind scientist everybody called "Prof" died on January 5, 1943. In 1946 the United States Congress named January 5th "George Washington Carver Day." He had given the world 300 ways to use the peanut and 118 ways to use the sweet potato.

24

Carver always took a bag on his walks so he could collect plant samples.

All through his life, Carver enjoyed painting and doing crafts such as knitting.

President Jimmy Carter, who was a peanut farmer from Georgia, said, "George Washington Carver was a great friend of the American farmer. He was a true genius."

26

George Washington Carver was a great scientist and inventor.

timeLine

1864(?) ~ Born in Diamond Grove, Missouri.

1877 ~ Begins school in Neosho, Missouri.

1884 ~ Attends high school in Minneapolis, Kansas.

1891 ~ Attends Iowa State College of Agricultural and Mechanical Arts.

1894 ~ Graduates from Iowa State College with a degree in agriculture; joins the staff.

1896 ~ Receives a master's degree in agriculture from Iowa State; becomes director of agriculture at Tuskegee Institute in Alabama.

1898 ~ Begins issuing bulletins about his experiments.

1918 ~ Becomes a consultant in agricultural research for the U.S. Department of Agriculture.

1923 ~ Is awarded the Spingarn Medal from the NAACP.

1939 ~ Opens George Washington Carver Museum in a ceremony with Henry Ford.

1943 ~ Dies on January 5 in Tuskegee, Alabama.

1894

1896

WORDS to KNOW

award—An honor given to a person for doing something special.

boll weevil—A small bug that kills cotton plants.

businessmen—Those who own a company, factory, or store.

college—A school beyond high school.

Congress—Government representatives and senators from each state who form a law-making body.

cowpea—A vegetable that is related to the black-eyed pea.

crop—The plants a farmer grows during one season.

crop rotation—Ways to rest the soil by not planting a crop on it for several years or by growing different crops.

goobers—An old African name for peanuts.

graduate—To finish all the studies at a school.

institute—a place of learning; a school.

Iowa State College—A college founded in 1858, now called Iowa State University of Science and Technology.

WORDS TO KNOW

lab—A short name for laboratory. A laboratory is a place where scientists work and study.

NAACP (National Association for the Advancement of Colored People)—An organization started to help all Americans gain equal rights and protection under the law.

president—The leader of a country or group.

professor—A name for a teacher who works at a college.

raiders—Another word for robbers.

scientist—A person who learns about a subject by asking questions and then trying to find answers.

slave—A person who is owned by another. A slave can be bought or sold.

stutter—To stumble over words.

Tuskegee Institute—A college founded in 1881 to teach African-American students. It is now called Tuskegee University.

wizard—A person who has great skill, talent, or knowledge.

Learn more about George Washington Carver

Books

Adler, David A. *A Picture Book of George Washington Carver.* New York, N.Y.: Holiday House, Inc., 1999.

Aliki. *A Weed Is a Flower: The Life of George Washington Carver.* New York, N.Y.: Simon & Schuster, 1991.

McLoone, Margo. *George Washington Carver.* Danbury, Conn.: Children's Press, 1997.

Mitchell, Barbara. *A Pocketful of Goobers: A Story About George Washington Carver.* Minneapolis, Minn.: The Lerner Publishing Group, 2000.

Internet Addresses

The Great Idea Finder: George Washington Carver
Fun facts and lots of links to other information.

<http://www.ideafinder.com/history/inventors/carver.htm>

Inventors Museum

<http://www.inventorsmuseum.com/georgecarver.htm>

Black History Inventors
Features an animation on crop rotation.

<http://www.tdo.com/local/bhm/bhinvent/bhinvent.htm>

index